Copyright © 2019

Rainey Leigh Seraphine

Wizzenhill Publishing

All rights reserved. Without limiting the rights under copyright reserved above, no part of this work/publication may be reproduced, stored in or introduced into a retrieval system, or transmitted, in any form or by any means electronic, mechanical, print, photocopying, recording or otherwise), without the prior written permission of the copyright owner.

ISBN 978-0-6485458-9-7

Another one!

For John and his little three legged dog, Piddling Pete!
He piddled on the ceiling
and he piddled on the floor
and when the butcher kicked him out
he piddled on the door!
John Gauld

For Helen and all the Gauld clan who would like to see
John's work as it should be,
a published book to treasure always.

It is an honour to work with this family!

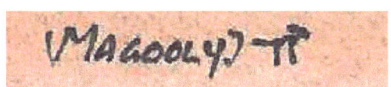

Look for his little dog in some of the following pictures!

Australian Natives

in

Lilting Limerick

Volume 2

Laughing Kookaburra

There once was a kooka called Burra,
whose laughing was shrill and quite thorough!
But when he tossed back his head,
it whacked a tree trunk instead!
Feeling dazed and confused,
and quite thoroughly bruised,
he fell off his branch,
in a bit of a trance,
and landed splat, right on top of his mother!
Poor Burra!

LAUGHING KOOKABURRA.
20·6·19.

Numbat

There once was a numbat called Norbert,
who was addictively fond of sweet sherbert!
In love with the fizz,
and the head spinning whizz,
his saliva would drool,
making great rocket fuel
for a sugar high planetary orbit!
Where's Norbert?

Numbat.
25·6·19.

Pacific Heron

There once was a heron called Sharon,
who met a young dude known as Warren!
She agreed to a date,
being eager to mate,
but the dude was quite lewd,
and impossibly rude,
so she flew off, alone and quite barren!
Poor Sharon!

Pacific Heron
22.6.19.

Pink Cockatoo

Drew was a pink cockatoo,
who desperately wished he was blue!
His life was a joke
as a pink Aussie bloke,
so he bought some blue paint,
for his feathers to taint,
but they all stuck together like glue!
Poor Drew!

Pink Cockatoo.
20.6.19

Spotted Quoll

There once was a black, spotted quoll,
who considered her humour quite droll!
When a joke she conspired,
made her keen and quite wired,
to deliver its end,
to her most loving friend,
met with nothing but yawns and an eye roll!
Poor quoll!

Quoll
24·6·19

Splendid Wren

A pretty young wren known as Suze,
was checking which suitor to choose!
But two who looked smart,
would unflinchingly fart
and the third who was Seth,
had the worst smelling breath!
So she joined all the nuns in recluse!
Poor Suze!

Splendid Wrens.
21·6·19.

Fairy Penguin

There was a plump penguin called Fairy,
whose brain was a bit light and airy!
With lacking the skill
to attract a boy, Wil
she decided to quit
at expanding her wit
and she joined Suze the wren's monastery!
Poor Fairy!

FAIRY PENGUIN.
23.6.19.

Eastern Grass Owl

There once was a grass owl called Bert,
who loved nothing more than to flirt!
It drove his wife nuts,
when he pinched all the butts
of some girls, who in outrage,
united in rampage,
pushed him out of his tree into dirt!
Poor Bert!

Eastern Grass Owl.
21.6.19.

Tasmanian Devil

There once was a devil called Neville,
who stupidly nipped his wife, Sheryl!
When she asked why he'd come,
to sink his teeth in her bum?
He answered her shrill,
'cause it gave him a thrill,
so her fry pan did leave him dishevelled!
Poor Neville!

Tasmanian Devil
22-6-19.

Galah

A galah known as Jacko's sweet wife,
found herself in some terrible strife!
She lost all his money,
when it fell down the dunny
and in panic she rushed,
but accidentally she flushed
and their riches are now not so rife!
Poor wife!

Galah. 21·6·19.

Field Mouse

There once was a field mouse called Flossie,
with a penchant to be loud and bossy!
When her husband rebelled,
with a wish for her quelled,
all she did was to smirk,
'cause she thought him a jerk!
So he left for Fiji, leaving Aussie!
Poor Flossie?

"Field Mouse". John Gauld. 28·6·19. (Magooly.)

Echidna

An echidna called Claire was a cutie
and the boys all would stare at her beauty!
When she wiggled her hips,
they all did backflips
and a brave boy in ardour,
wished to visit her parlour,
snuggled up and got pricked by her bootie!
Poor boy!

"Echidna."

John Gauld. 6·7·19.
(Magooly)

Huntsman Spider

There once was a huntsman called Rodger,
an excessively hairy old codger!
Who refused his wife's pleas,
to at least shave his knees,
'cause they tickled her butt,
when they lay in their hut,
so with razor in hand,
she took one mighty stand
and poor Roger failed badly to dodge her!
Poor Roger!

"Huntsman Spider".

John. Gauld. 7.7.19.
(Maroocy.)

Other books by Rainey Leigh Seraphine:

We're Off to the Moon in My Hot Air Balloon
Miranda Merbaby's Mystical World
Wicky the Wacky Witch & Grumpy Mr Whilloby
Bronte's Book
Our Dad Hates Bugs
The Snowflake Who Wouldn't Fall
Where is the Easter Bunny
The Fairies Tale
Aristotle The Rebel
Theo's World (about Dwarfism)
Skiddy Squirrel's Poetically Preposterous Account of
Awesome Animal Antics
Greta's Dilemma
The Pappinbarra Flood
Bonny Bilby
Australian Natives in Lilting Limerick Volume 1

Available at all online bookstores and retail outlets.

Visit: www.raineyleighseraphine.com
or author's Facebook page: raineyleighseraphine

www.ingramcontent.com/pod-product-compliance
Lightning Source LLC
Chambersburg PA
CBHW042144290426
44110CB00002B/104